heals

illustrated by Gordon Stowell

Jesus healed a lot of people. He taught that God loves us and knows all about us. Here are two stories about how Jesus made people better.

An important man called Jairus had a daughter aged twelve. She was very ill. "I will go and ask Jesus to help," he thought.

Shortly after Jairus had spoken to
Jesus a messenger came to tell him
that his child had died.

"Do not be afraid," said Jesus. "All is well."

Jesus went to Jairus' house. He told the people that the little girl was only asleep.

They all laughed at him. "The little girl is dead," they said.

Taking her by the hand, Jesus said, "Little girl, get up now." And immediately she sat up. "Look," said Jesus. "She is hungry, give her some food." Everyone was astonished.

There was once a man who could not walk. He had four good friends. One day Jesus came into their village. The friends decided to take their friend to be healed.

Jesus was talking to a great crowd of people in a house. "We'll never get in to see Him," said the poor man.

"Just look! We cannot even see the
door there are so many people!"

"No," said his friends. "We'll not get in through the door, but there is another way."

They hurried up the steps at the side
of the house and got onto the roof.
Quickly they pulled up the roof tiles
and made a big hole.

They fastened ropes round their
friend and lowered him down

. . . right to the feet of Jesus.

Jesus looked at him. "You are
forgiven," He said. "Take up your
bed and walk."

The man found suddenly that he
could move. He leapt to his feet,
rolled up his bed and danced away.
A wonderful thing had happened

to him that day, and he praised God for it.

The story of Jairus is in Matthew chapter 9, verses 18–26, and the Four Good Friends is in Luke chapter 5, verses 17–26.

Little Fish Books about Jesus

JESUS is born

Little Fish Books about Jesus

JESUS heals

Little Fish Books about Jesus

JESUS teaches

Little Fish Books about Jesus

JESUS loves

 Little Fish Books